This Book will help you get organized, and when the time comes, it will be a huge benefit to your loved ones.   You will use it to compile and record everything that your survivors need to know, including personal, financial and legal information and document locations, as well as your final wishes and arrangements.

Who should plan ahead?   <u>**Every adult**</u> can benefit from the Yup I'm Dead...Now What? Planner.

Getting started is easy.

Download the Quick Start Guide at CaringHub.net/quick-start/

CaringHub will walk you through the process in 30 days or less.

<u>**Connect with us:**</u>

<u>www.CaringHub.net</u>

Question?   CaringHub.net/contact/

Facebook.com/caringhub

Pinterest.com/caringhub

You can remove this page and keep for your records.

THIS BOOK BELONGS TO:

CONTACT INFORMATION:

DATE LAST UPDATED:

YUP I'M DEAD...
NOW WHAT?

A Guide to My Life Information, Documents, Plans and Final Wishes

"Our most basic common link is that we all inhabit this planet. We all breathe the same air. We all cherish our children's future. And we are all mortal."
– John F. Kennedy

Dear Family and Friends,

It wasn't until my Grandmother died and I become a Mother myself, that I realized when it comes to our family, we want to be sure they are protected and prepared for whatever life brings them. There are so many things we need to remember. It is virtually impossible to remember everything we need to without writing it down somewhere. The problem for many of us is that we try to keep all the information in our own head, in files, or we write things down on slips of paper that are scattered everywhere that no one understands but us *(and even we find notes that we wrote and we no longer have a clue what they were about)*!

If something was to happen to me, I did not want my family to have to have to worry about pulling all this information together. Also, as a member of the *"sandwich generation"*, I did not feel comfortable asking my Parents and In-Laws tough questions about their personal, medical, financial records and end of life wishes. It's just a difficult issue that *(while everyone has to deal with it)*...not many wish to talk to about it.

That is why I set out to create **Yup I'm Dead...Now What?** This Book/Planner is a valuable resource and gift to loved ones that will guide you through the process of ***getting your crap together so your family doesn't have to!*** My goal was to give you one source to record valuable, personal information that you can have in your home and/or share with loved ones. I also wanted my family to know what to expect, and what to do, when the time comes for me to drop *Dead as a Doornail*. Knowing that this will be one of the most difficult times for my children, I wanted to keep this Book "light hearted", and I surely do not want to contribute to their stress and frustration by leaving my life memories, important records and final wishes spread all over the place. I wanted my personal information and final wishes compiled in one location where they can easily turn to when the time comes. It will guide them through the first days, weeks and months following your departure.

Yup I'm Dead...Now What? will provide those you love with the information they need to handle the practical aspects of your Death. If possible, we recommend you sit down with your family and review the information you've entered, so they know what to expect when the time comes.

While nobody wants to contemplate his or her own death, you can give your loved ones a certain amount of peace of mind by maintaining an updated will, investing in some life insurance, and completing this

Planner, which will provide support and guidance regarding your final wishes when your family needs it most. My hope is that by using this Planner, you will be able to spend more time enjoying your family and less time searching for records and worrying about end of life decisions!

To my Grandmother, Maggie, I love and miss you every day. You have inspired me to write this guide for two reasons:

The first being...to be sure my crap is in order, so my kids aren't struggling to read and decipher all my notes (like you wrote and left around the house).

The second being....to give guidance for end of life wishes so my family has a roadmap to abide by.

I want them to know how much I love them and my final wishes and words for them.

Fill out and give to Loved Ones to let them know you have the

Yup I'm Dead..Now What? Planner when your Planner is complete.

Make copies if additional are needed if you need more than two.

Dear _____,

I have completed Yup I'm Dead...Now What? Planner which contains details about my Life Information, Documents, Plans and Final Wishes.   When the time comes for me to *leave this joint*, this Book will be your guide through the days, weeks, and months following my departure.   You can find the Book in this location:

_____

Turn to Chapter 1 immediately following my departure.   It will be your guide.   You will also find information regarding my Final Wishes, Key Contacts, and Important Documents.

_____

Signature   Date

   Be sure to keep this note in a safe, secure place that you can access when needed

---

Dear _____,

I have completed Yup I'm Dead...Now What? Planner which contains details about my Life Information, Documents, Plans and Final Wishes.   When the time comes for me to *leave this joint*, this Book will be your guide through the days, weeks, and months following my departure.   You can find the Book in this location:

_____

Turn to Chapter 1 immediately following my departure.   It will be your guide.   You will also find information regarding my Final Wishes, Key Contacts, and Important Documents.

_____

Signature   Date

   Be sure to keep this note in a safe, secure place that you can access when needed

Contents

What the "Yup I'm Dead...Now What?" Planner Contains

This Planner will guide you through the 30 topics listed below.   For many of the topics, you will find that you have related documents such as: birth or marriage certificates, a will, trust, or power of attorney, insurance policies, that you will need to locate.   You will find a "Where to Find It" Master Document in Chapter 1, as well as in the applicable Chapter.   If possible, you should file them in one location or with your Planner.   Your Planner is a handy organizational tool that offers you ease of access, as well as a valuable resource for caretakers and survivors.

1. **Instructions:**   In this section, you will find instructions for the first few days, weeks, and months following your incapacity and death.   This will include a "Where to Find It" Master Document for ease of locating all important Documents in one location.   This will be of great value to your loved ones.

2. **Letter to Family and Loved Ones:**   A personal letter, written to your beloved family and caregivers.   The letter is one of the first things your survivors will read when they turn to your Planner after your death.

3. **Personal Information:**   Facts and vital statistics about your life and family members, and the locations of important documents such as birth, marriage, and death certificates.

4. **Medical Information**: Important health forms, medical conditions, health insurance, primary physician and specialists, hospital and what needs to be done if I am not able to care for myself.

5. **Key Contacts:**   Executor, attorney, accountant, financial advisor, insurance agents.

6. **Time of My Passing:**   People to contact when I'm Dead as a Doornail.

7. **My Dependents:**   Information about my dependents and instructions for their care.

8. **Pets:**   Information, instructions and wishes for pet care.

9. **Important Documents:**   Health care documents, power of attorney, will and trust, driver's license, and passport, birth certificate, and marriage certificate locations.

10. **Financial Information:**   Financial power of attorney, bank accounts, credit and debit cards, investments, tax records, safe deposit box, what I owe, what is owed to me.

11. **Retirement Plans and Pensions:**   Information about any retirement accounts or pension benefits to which you are entitled, including the location of these documents.

12. **Government Benefits:**   Information about Social Security or other government benefits to which you are entitled.

13. **Commercial/Business Information:** About my Business.

14. **Memberships and Organizations**:   A summary of memberships and organizations that I am involved in, including contact or login information and any accrued benefits.

15. **Beneficiaries:**   What Beneficiaries can expect....Life insurance, Employer Benefits, Social Security, Pensions, Veteran's Benefits.

16. **Personal Property:**   Residence, real estate, commercial property, vehicles, heirlooms, personal items, firearms, storage unit, safe, safe deposit box.

17. **Insurance:**   Life, home, rental, health, vehicle, other.

18. **What to Pay, Close, Cancel:**   Utilities, cell phone, cable, internet, auto pay accounts, charities, subscriptions, memberships, etc.
19. **Email and Social Media:**   Usernames and passwords for email and social media accounts, websites and blogs.
20. **Secured Places and Passwords:**   All the places you keep under lock and key (or protect by password), including safe deposit boxes, property and vehicle alarms, and password-protected software devices or accounts
21. **Organ or Body Donation:**   Wishes and plans for donation of your body, organs, and tissues, including the location of related documents.
22. **Burial or Cremation:**   Wishes and plans for burial or cremation, including the location of any related documents.
23. **Funeral and Memorial Services:**   Wishes and plans for a viewing, visitation, wake, funeral, memorial, or other service, including the locations of important documents.
24. **Obituary:**   An obituary you've written for a newspaper or other publication, or details you'd like your survivors to include if they write your obituary.
25. **Will and Trust:**   Information about your will and other estate planning documents, such as trusts. You can also include details about any documents that affect how your property will be dispersed after death, such as a prenuptial agreement.
26. **Miscellaneous Information:**   Anything else you want to include in your Planner or that you want your survivors to know about.
27. **Miscellaneous Contacts:**   Any other miscellaneous contacts and information you would like them to know or receive.
28. **Service Providers:**   Contact information for your current service providers, including medical, dental, personal care, property care, and others.
29. **Personal Wishes:**   My wishes outlined here.
30. **Last Words:**   My last words here.

Feel free to remove these pages after your Planner is complete.

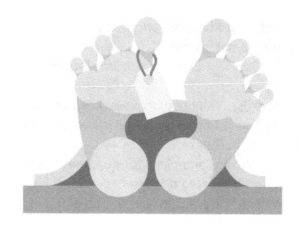

YUP I'M DEAD..
NOW WHAT?

Name	
Date	

Yup I'm Dead and you're probably wondering what to do.

Don't worry……this Book will be your Guide.

Turn to **Chapter 1**, *Instructions*, for what to do and when.

Chapter 1

Instructions

Chapter 1 is the **Road Map to Important Information about My Belongings and Wishes.** It is organized to help guide you through the next few days, weeks, and months—outlining what you need to do and where you will find the information you need.

Most of the tasks will apply if I am _Dead as a Doornail_ or _incapacitated and not able to make decisions for myself_ —though how you handle a task may vary depending upon the circumstances.   (I know – fun stuff, right?)

"Incapacitated" is such as harsh word.   If you are reading this, chances are, you are probably upset and emotional.   We certainly do not want to make it worse for you, and are trying to keep this book as "up beat" as possible while you navigate this difficult time.   From this point forward I will refer to "Incapacitated" as "Zombified".

Yeah, yeah, yeah, I know.   You may not agree with this.

However, I don't want you to be sad, and I am trying to make this as easy for you as possible!

First, if I am Zombified, there are two important tasks:

If I Am Zombified

1. Review Health Care Directives   Applicable: Yes ____   No ____

❑ **Health Care Directives.**   Turn to Chapter 9 for information about documents I have made to direct my health care.

2. Review Power of Attorney for Finances   Applicable: Yes ____   No ____

❑ **Durable Power of Attorney for Finances.**   Turn to Chapter 9 for information about the document that names someone to manage my finances for me.

➢ Now follow this Guide for **Days 1 and 2**— whether I am **Zombified** or am **Dead as a Doornail.**
➢ Next week, complete the tasks in **Week 2**.
➢ Within the next month, get started on the tasks in **Month 1 and Beyond**.

Days 1 and 2

These are some of the important tasks you will need to handle in the first 48 hours following my Zombification or Death.

Care for Children   Applicable: Yes ____   No ____
❑ **Children.**   Turn to Chapter 7 for details about the children who rely on me for care.

Care for Others   Applicable: Yes ____   No ____
❑ **Others who Depend on Me.**   Turn to Chapter 7 for details about other people who rely on me for care.

Care for Animals   Applicable: Yes____   No ____

❑ **Pets.**   Turn to Chapter 8 for information about taking care of my animals, including my wishes for placing them with others.

Contact Employer   Applicable: Yes____   No ____
❑ **Employment.**   Notify my employer of my incapacity or death. See Chapter 6 for contact information and other details about my current employer.

<u>**Contact Business**</u>   Applicable: Yes___   No ___

- ☐ **Business Interests.**   Notify any business partners or key employees of my Zombification or Death. See Chapter 13 for contact information and details about my business interests.

<u>Make Final Arrangements</u>

After I'm Dead as a Doornail, please review these five items before making any final arrangements.

- ☐ **Arrange for the Death Certificate.** Those in charge of handling my estate will need certified copies of my death certificate to wrap up business with Insurance Companies, Banks, the Social Security Administration, and others.

  As you make arrangements for the burial, cremation, or whatever my wishes are, you will be asked to provide information for the death certificate. The Personal Information (Chapter 3) contains the information you will need. At this time, you should request multiple certified copies of the death certificate; you may up to 10 copies.

  If you are unable to request copies of my death certificate while making final arrangements, you can get them later. To find out where to send your request, go to the National Center for Health Statistics website, www.cdc.gov/nchs/w2w/index.htm, and click the link for the state where I died.

- ☐ **Organ or Body Donation.** Turn to Chapter 21 for my wishes about donating my body, organs, or tissues—as well as information about any plans I have already made.

- ☐ **Burial or Cremation.** Turn to Chapter 22 for details about burial or cremation, including my wishes and information about any plans I have already made.

- ☐ **Funeral and Memorial Services.** Turn to Chapter 23 for details about my funeral, memorial, or related services, including my wishes and information about any plans I have already made.

- ☐ **Obituary.** Turn to Chapter 24 for details about publishing my obituary.

<u>Contact Family and Friends</u>

- ☐ Contact all friends and relatives who I have listed in Chapter 5 and if there is anyone else who I may have missed that should know of my Zombification or Death.

  If you will hold a funeral or memorial service in the next few days, contact everyone who may attend. Others will learn of my passing only by reading the obituary, if I have chosen to have one published.

  Except for those who need to know about my death right away, it will help to make any arrangements for services before you make phone calls—then you won't have to call everyone twice.

You can find names and contact information for family and friends in the following locations:

_____

_____

_____

_____

❏ **Protect the House.** My obituary or death notice may serve to alert thieves that the house is empty. If necessary, arrange for a neighbor, a familiar service provider, a church member, or other close friend or family member to be at the house during services.

Review Appointment Calendar

❏ Review my calendar and cancel any scheduled appointments. You can find my calendar in the following locations:

_____

_____

Manage Mail and Newspaper

❏ Pick up my mail. See Chapter 3 for access information, if needed. File a mail forwarding order with USPS.

❏ Cancel my newspaper subscriptions, if any. See Chapter 16 for payment and account information.

Read My Last Letters

❏ **Letter to Loved Ones.** As time permits, please see Chapter 2 and 30 for my last letters to those closest to me.

Additional Notes:

_____

_____

_____

_____

_____

_____

Week 2

This Chapter outlines the essential tasks you should handle in the two weeks following my Zombification or Death.

Locate my Will or Other Estate Planning Documents

☐ **Will and Trust.**   After my death, see Chapter 25 for information about my will, trusts, or other estate planning documents that I have made.

Contact Organizations and Service Providers

Please notify financial institutions, brokers, government agencies, and others with whom I do business that I have become Zombified or Dead as a Doornail. The following Chapters will help you:

☐ **Insurance.**   Turn to Chapter 17 for information about my insurance agents and policies. The information there will help you claim benefits, cancel, or continue coverage as appropriate.

☐ **Bank Accounts.**   Turn to Chapter 10 for financial institution contact information and details about my bank and brokerage accounts.

☐ **Retirement Plans and Pensions.**   Turn to Chapter 11 for information about my retirement and pension plan accounts, including contact information for the administrators.

☐ **Government Benefits.**   Turn to Chapter 12 for details about my Social Security and other government benefits, including contact information for each agency.

☐ **Service Providers.**   Turn to Chapter 10 and 28 for information about service providers, including medical, personal, and household care providers.

☐ **Other:**

_____

_____

_____

☐ **Other:**

_____

_____

_____

_____

Review Current Bills and Accounts

☐ **Credit Cards and Debts.** Please review my current bills to be sure they are paid on time. Cancel and close accounts as necessary. See Chapter 10 for more information.

☐ **Secured Places and Passwords.** Turn to Chapter 20 for help with locked or password-protected products, services, and accounts.

Additional Notes:

_____

_____

_____

_____

_____

_____

_____

_____

Whether my death was sudden or a long time coming, you will experience loss after I'm gone. You may grieve for weeks, months, or even years. Grieving is unique, normal and personal. You may not grieve the same as other family members or friends. A Brother and Sister may grieve completely different. One may be devastated and find it difficult to function. The other may try to distract themselves and go about their daily activities. This is completely normal. Everyone is different and their grieving and coping mechanisms are completely normal and unique to their self and situation.

During the grieving process, it is normal to feel strong emotions, such as deep sadness, confusion, despair, or anger. You may even go through a time of depression. You will heal more quickly if you share your grief with supportive people—family members, friends, your faith community, therapists or grief support groups. To find a local group (and helpful information) consult your health care providers or visit these organizations online:

- Open to Hope (www.opentohope.com)
- Legacy Connect (www.connect.legacy.com)
- National Alliance for Grieving Children (www.childrengrieve.org)

Month 1 and Beyond

The following is a list of tasks that you should initiate in the first month or two following my Zombification or Death.

Take Inventory

- ❑ **Real Estate.** Turn to Chapter 16 for details about any real estate that I own or rent.
- ❑ **Vehicles.** Turn to Chapter 16 for information about all vehicles that I own.
- ❑ **Other Income and Personal Property.** Turn to Chapter 16 for information about important sources of income or items of personal property not described elsewhere in my planner.
- ❑ **Other Information.** See Chapter 16 for any other details that I feel you need to know.

Cancel Memberships and Driver's License

- ❑ **Memberships and Communities.** Over time, you will want to cancel my memberships with various organizations. See Chapter 14 for contact information.
- ❑ **Driver's License.** Notify the state motor vehicles department of my death and cancel my license. See Chapter 3 for my driver's license information. Also, please turn in my handicap placard, if I had one.

Prepare Tax Returns

☐ **Taxes.** Chapter 10 will help you gather the information you need to prepare my final tax returns. Keep returns and related records for seven years.

Additional Notes:

_____

_____

_____

_____

_____

_____

_____

Where to Get Help

As you work through the steps you must take to wrap up my affairs, you will find a number of sources for help. Where applicable, the various Chapters of This Guide list lawyers, accountants, or others who can help with each task.

Additional resources you can turn to include:
- Your primary health care provider
- A community-based bereavement program or hospice service
- Counseling services
- A faith group
- Trustworthy friends and family members
- Web-based support services for people in bereavement

WHERE TO FIND IT MASTER LIST

Name:_____ Social Security #: _____

Spouse/Partner name:_____ Social Security #: _____

Address:_____

Date prepared:_____ Copies given to: _____

My valuable papers are stored in these LOCATIONS (address or where to look):

A: **Residence:** _____

B: **Safe Deposit Box:** _____

C: **Other:** _____

ITEM	LOCATION A	B	C	ITEM	LOCATION A	B	C
My will (original)	☐	☐	☐	Retirement papers	☐	☐	☐
Advance Health Directive/Living Will	☐	☐	☐	Retirement accounts (IRA, 401K, etc.)	☐	☐	☐
Power of Attorney — healthcare	☐	☐	☐	Funeral arrangements	☐	☐	☐
Power of Attorney — finance	☐	☐	☐	Titles and deeds	☐	☐	☐
Spouse's/partner's will (original)	☐	☐	☐	Notes (mortgages)	☐	☐	☐
Safe combination	☐	☐	☐	List of stored and loaned items	☐	☐	☐
Trust agreement	☐	☐	☐	Auto ownership records	☐	☐	☐
Life insurance policy(s)	☐	☐	☐	Birth certificate	☐	☐	☐
Health insurance policy(s)	☐	☐	☐	Military/veteran's papers	☐	☐	☐
Long-term care insurance	☐	☐	☐	Marriage certificate	☐	☐	☐
Car insurance policy	☐	☐	☐	Children's birth certificates	☐	☐	☐
Homeowner/rental policy	☐	☐	☐	Divorce/separation records	☐	☐	☐
Employment contracts	☐	☐	☐	Passwords (important websites,			
Partnership agreements	☐	☐	☐	banking, credit card, social media,			
List of checking, savings account	☐	☐	☐	computer, wi-fi, phone, etc.)	☐	☐	☐
List of credit cards and numbers	☐	☐	☐	Safe deposit box key	☐	☐	☐
List of important friends/neighbors	☐	☐	☐	Other _____	☐	☐	☐

Emergency contact: _____

Doctor(s):_____

Clergy:_____

Attorney:_____

Accountant:_____

Insurance agent/policy #(s): _____

Other contacts: _____

In Chapter 2, you will find my letter to You, Family Members and Loved Ones.

This will most likely be one of the first things you read and you will most likely be sad, confused and emotional.

Read more about Grief and what you can do to help yourself here:

https://caringhub.net/what-is-grief/

Chapter 2
Letter to Family and Loved Ones

If you're reading this, it is because I am Zombified or Dead as a Doornail.

To:

_____

_____

_____

_____

_____

Thoughts about My Death

_____

_____

_____

_____

_____

_____

_____

_____

Messages for My Loved Ones

_____

_____

_____

_____

_____

_____

_____

_____

_____

My Last Words to You

_____

_____

_____

Signature

_____

Chapter 3
Personal Information

In this Chapter, you will find important personal information about me and those closest to me. You may need these vital statistics for a number of tasks, such as preparing my death certificate, writing my obituary, filing tax returns, and distributing assets to my beneficiaries.

Legal Name: _____

Maiden Name: _____

Address: _____

_____

_____

Residence of City Since (year): _____

Residence of State Since (year): _____

PO Box No: _____

PO Box Key Location: _____

Phone No: _____

Cell No: _____

Social Security No: _____

My Social Security Card is Located: _____

Driver's License No and State: _____

Maiden Name: _____

Date of Birth: _____

Location of Birth Certificate: _____

Birthplace: _____

_____

Schools attended/dates: _____

_____

Colleges attended/dates: _____

_____

Marital Status: _____

Date of Marriage: _____

Location of Marriage Certificate: _____

Spouse's Name: _____

Date of Divorce, Separation or Death: _____

Location of Documents: _____

Children's Name(s) and DOB: _____

_____

_____

Grandchildren's Name(s) and DOB: _____

_____

_____

My Former Spouse's Name: _____

_____

_____

My Sibling's Names:_____

_____

_____

My Father's Name:_____

_____

My Father's Birthplace:_____

_____

My Mother's Maiden Name:_____

_____

My Mother's Birthplace:_____

_____

Notes:

_____

_____

_____

_____

Occupation: _____

Citizenship Info: _____

Religious Organizations to which I belong: _____

_____

_____

Military Service: _____

_____

_____

Location of Military Documents: _____

What I remember about my Grandparents: _____

_____

_____

_____

_____

_____

_____

_____

_____

_____

_____

_____

_____

What I remember about my Childhood: _____

_____

_____

_____

_____

_____

Additional Memories and Notes:_____

_____

_____

_____

_____

_____

_____

_____

Family Items of Importance, Location and Notes:_____

_____

Chapter 4

MEDICAL

In this Chapter, you will find Information about documents I have made, about my Medical History and about how direct my Health Care if I am Zombified.

My Living Will is located: _____

_____

My Health Care Power of Attorney is located: _____

_____

My Appointed Agent is: _____

_____

Alternate #1 is: _____

Alternate #2 is: _____

My DNR/Do Not Resuscitate Order is located: _____

_____

I will _____ or I will not _____ be donating my organs_____

My organ donation/anatomical gift information is located: _____

_____

_____

Blood Type: _____

Medical Conditions: _____

_____

_____

_____

_____

_____

_____

Medications: _____

_____

_____

_____

_____

_____

Allergies and Reactions: _____

_____

_____

_____

_____

_____

_____

_____

Health Insurance Info: _____

_____

_____

My Health Insurance Card is Located: _____

_____

_____

Primary Care Physician:_____

_____

Contact Information: _____

_____

_____

Preferred Hospital:_____

Location and Contact Info:_____

_____

_____

Preferred Pharmacy: _____

_____

Location and Contact Info: _____

_____

Other Medical Specialists: _____

Contact Information: _____

_____

Other Medical Specialists: _____

Contact Information: _____

_____

Other Medical Specialists: _____

Contact Information: _____

_____

Things to be taken care of if I am Zombified and not able to do them myself: _____

_____

_____

_____

_____

_____

_____

_____

_____

_____

Notes:

_____

_____

_____

_____

Chapter 5
KEY CONTACTS

These are the people you will need to contact right away when I'm Dead or Zombified.

Executor:_____

Contact Information:_____

_____

_____

Attorney: _____

Contact Information: _____

_____

_____

Accountant:_____

Contact Information: _____

_____

_____

Tax Preparer:_____

Contact Information: _____

_____

_____

Financial Advisor:_____

Contact Information: _____

_____

_____

Insurance Agent:_____

Contact Information: _____

_____

_____

Primary Care Provider:_____

Contact Information: _____

_____

_____

Other Health Care Provider: _____

Contact Information: _____

_____

_____

Other Health Care Provider: _____

Contact Information: _____

_____

_____

Other Health Care Provider: _____

Contact Information: _____

_____

_____

Other Health Care Provider: _____

Contact Information: _____

_____

_____

Other Health Care Provider: _____

Contact Information: _____

_____

_____

Other Health Care Provider: _____

Contact Information: _____

_____

_____

Other Health Care Provider: _____

Contact Information: _____

_____

_____

Clergy Person:_____

Contact Information: _____

_____

_____

Other: _____

_____

_____

_____

_____

Notes: _____

_____

_____

_____

_____

_____

_____

_____

_____

_____

_____

_____

Chapter 6

Time of My Passing

Now that I'm dead, you will need to request 10 copies of the death certificate for legal purposes, insurance, etc., and please contact the following individuals:

Family Member: _____

Contact Information:_____

_____

Family Member: _____

Contact Information:_____

_____

Family Member: _____

Contact Information:_____

_____

Family Member: _____

Contact Information:_____

_____

Family Member: _____

Contact Information:_____

_____

Family Member: _____

Contact Information:_____

_____

Family Member: _____

Contact Information:_____

_____

Family Member: _____

Contact Information:_____

_____

Family Member: _____

Contact Information:_____

_____

Family Member: _____

Contact Information:_____

_____

Friend: _____

Contact Information:_____

_____

Friend: _____

Contact Information:_____

_____

Friend: _____

Contact Information:_____

_____

Friend: _____

Contact Information:_____

_____

Friend: _____

Contact Information:_____

_____

Friend: _____

Contact Information:_____

_____

Friend: _____

Contact Information:_____

_____

Friend: _____

Contact Information:_____

_____

Friend: _____

Contact Information:_____

_____

Friend: _____

Contact Information:_____

_____

Friend: _____

Contact Information:_____

_____

Friend: _____

Contact Information:_____

_____

Friend: _____

Contact Information:_____

_____

Friend: _____

Contact Information:_____

_____

Friend: _____

Contact Information:_____

_____

Friend: _____

Contact Information:_____

_____

My Employer:

_____

Contact Information:_____

_____

Others: _____

Contact Information:_____

_____

Others: _____

Contact Information:_____

_____

Others: _____

Contact Information:_____

_____

Others: _____

Contact Information:_____

_____

Others: _____

Contact Information:_____

_____

Others: _____

Contact Information:_____

Notes:_____

_____

_____

_____

_____

_____

_____

_____

_____

_____

_____

_____

_____

_____

_____

_____

Chapter 7

My Dependents

This is where you will find information about my children, aging parents or other dependents here.

Name:_____

Relationship:_____

Residence and Contact Info: _____

_____

Birthdate and Birthplace:_____

Citizenship: _____

Other Personal Information: _____

Caregiver, Custody or Guardianship Information: _____

_____

Location of Documents:_____

_____

Health and Medical Information: _____

_____

Conditions: _____

_____

Allergies: _____

_____

Health Care Providers: _____

_____

Health Insurance Information: _____

_____

Financial Information: _____

Location of Documents: _____

_____

Notes and Instructions for Care: _____

_____

_____

_____

Other Valuable Information: _____

_____

_____

_____

_____

_____

_____

_____

_____

Name:_____

Relationship:_____

Residence and Contact Info: _____

_____

Birthdate and Birthplace:_____

Citizenship: _____

Other Personal Information: _____

Caregiver, Custody or Guardianship Information: _____

_____

Location of Documents:_____

_____

Health and Medical Information: _____

_____

Conditions: _____

_____

Allergies: _____

_____

Health Care Providers: _____

_____

Health Insurance Information: _____

_____

Financial Information: _____

Location of Documents: _____

_____

Notes and Instructions for Care: _____

_____

_____

_____

Other Valuable Information: _____

_____

_____

_____

_____

_____

_____

_____

_____

Name:_____

Relationship:_____

Residence and Contact Info: _____

_____

Birthdate and Birthplace:_____

Citizenship: _____

Other Personal Information: _____

Caregiver, Custody or Guardianship Information: _____

_____

Location of Documents:_____

_____

Health and Medical Information: _____

_____

Conditions: _____

_____

Allergies: _____

_____

Health Care Providers: _____

_____

Health Insurance Information: _____

_____

Financial Information: _____

Location of Documents: _____

_____

Notes and Instructions for Care: _____

_____

_____

_____

Other Valuable Information: _____

_____

_____

_____

_____

_____

Name:_____

Relationship:_____

Residence and Contact Info: _____

_____

Birthdate and Birthplace:_____

Citizenship: _____

Other Personal Information: _____

Caregiver, Custody or Guardianship Information: _____

_____

Location of Documents:_____

_____

Health and Medical Information: _____

_____

Conditions: _____

_____

Allergies: _____

_____

Health Care Providers: _____

_____

Health Insurance Information: _____

_____

Financial Information: _____

Location of Documents: _____

_____

Notes and Instructions for Care: _____

_____

_____

_____

Other Valuable Information: _____

_____

Chapter 8

Pets

This chapter describes my wishes for my Pets care and placement.

MY PETS

Pet Name: _____

Description/Age: _____

_____

License/ID Info: _____

Health Info: _____

_____

Veterinarian: _____

_____

Who will care for my Pet: _____

Name: _____

Contact Info: _____

_____

Instructions for caring for my Pet: _____

_____

_____

_____

Pet Name: _____

Description/Age: _____

_____

License/ID Info: _____

Health Info: _____

_____

Veterinarian: _____

_____

Who will care for my Pet: _____

Name: _____

Contact Info: _____

_____

Instructions for caring for my Pet: _____

_____

_____

_____

Pet Name: _____

Description/Age: _____

_____

License/ID Info: _____

Health Info: _____

_____

Veterinarian: _____

_____

Who will care for my Pet: _____

Name: _____

Contact Info: _____

_____

Instructions for caring for my Pet: _____

_____

_____

_____

Pet Name: _____

Description/Age: _____

_____

License/ID Info: _____

Health Info: _____

_____

Veterinarian: _____

_____

Who will care for my Pet: _____

Name: _____

Contact Info: _____

_____

Instructions for caring for my Pet: _____

_____

_____

_____

Pet Name: _____

Description/Age: _____

_____

License/ID Info: _____

Health Info: _____

_____

Veterinarian: _____

_____

Who will care for my Pet: _____

Name: _____

Contact Info:_____

Chapter 9

Important Documents

Now that I'm Dead, you will need to locate my Important Documents. This section provides details about these documents and where you can find them. If an attorney or other professional (such as a tax expert) helped me prepare a document listed here, I have included contact information for him or her. You can consult the professional if you have questions about the document or need help carrying out its terms.

Health Care Agent

In my health care documents, I have named the person listed below to be my health care agent. My agent will supervise my care if I am incapacitated. If he or she is unable to serve, I have named alternates to serve in the order listed.

Health Care Agent	
Alternate 1	
Alternate 2	
Alternate 3	

Health Care Documents

Following is basic information about my health care documents. If an attorney or other professional helped me prepare a document listed here, I have included contact information for him or her. You can consult the listed professional if you have questions about the document or need help carrying out its terms.

Document Title	
Date Prepared	
Effective Date	[ ] Immediately [ ] Upon my incapacity [ ] Other:
Professional Help	An attorney or other professional helped me prepare this document: [ ] Yes [ ] No
Professional's Name, Title, and Contact Information	

Location of Original Document	
Locations of Copies of This Document	
Additional Notes	

Durable Power of Attorney for Finances

The following document is durable, which means it remains effective after I am incapacitated and unable to manage my own affairs. All powers granted under the document terminate upon my death. For information about who has authority to handle my affairs after death, see following pages, Will and Trust.

Document Title	
Date Prepared	
Agent's Name	
Alternate Agents' Names	
Effective Date	[ ] Immediately [ ] Upon my incapacity [ ] Other:
Professional Help	An attorney or other professional helped me prepare this document: [ ] Yes [ ] No
Professional's Name, Title, and Contact Information	
Location of Original Document	
Locations of Copies of This Document	

Additional Notes	

Other Financial Power of Attorney

The following documents are not durable, which means that they are no longer valid if I become incapacitated. If possible, please locate and destroy all copies of these documents to prevent anyone from mistakenly taking action under them.

Document Title	
Date Prepared	
Agent's Name	
Alternate Agents' Names	
Effective Date	[ ] Immediately [ ] Other:
Termination Date	[ ] Upon my incapacity or death [ ] Other:
Professional Help	An attorney or other professional helped me prepare this document: [ ] Yes [ ] No
Professional's Name, Title, and Contact Information	
Location of Original Document	
Locations of Copies of This Document	
Additional Notes	

Will and Trust

Document Title	
Date Prepared	
Professional Help	An attorney or other professional helped me prepare this document: [ ] Yes [ ] No
Professional's Name, Title, and Contact Information	
Location of Original Document	
Locations of Copies of This Document	
Executor or Successor Trustee	
Alternate 1	
Alternate 2	
Additional Notes	

Document Title	
Date Prepared	
Professional Help	An attorney or other professional helped me prepare this document: [ ] Yes [ ] No
Professional's Name, Title, and Contact Information	

Location of Original Document	
Locations of Copies of This Document	
Executor or Successor Trustee	
Alternate 1	
Alternate 2	
Additional Notes	

Other Important Documents:

My Driver's License is located: _____

_____

My Driver's License Number: _____

_____

My Passport is located: _____

My Passport Number is: _____

My Birth Certificate is Located: _____

My Marriage Certificate is Located: _____

My Divorce Papers are Located: _____

Information on my Computer:

Usernames and Passwords:_____

_____

_____

_____

Notes regarding other documents: _____

_____

_____

_____

_____

_____

_____

_____

_____

Chapter 10
Financial Information

Yup, I'm dead and you will need to know about Financial appointments, accounts and records.

My Financial Power of Attorney Document is Located: _____

_____

My Appointed Agent is: _____

_____

BANK ACCOUNT INFORMATION

Checking Account: _____

Bank: _____

Account No: _____

Online Acct Username: _____

Password: _____

Savings Account: _____

Bank: _____

Account No: _____

Online Acct Username: _____

Password: _____

Other Accounts: _____

Bank: _____

Account No: _____

Online Acct Username: _____

Password: _____

Other Account: _____

Bank: _____

Account No: _____

Online Acct Username: _____

Password: _____

Other Account: _____

Bank: _____

Account No: _____

Online Acct Username: _____

Password: _____

ATM Card: _____

Bank: _____

Account No: _____

PIN: _____

Debit Card: _____

Bank: _____

Account No: _____

PIN: _____

Notes:

_____

_____

CREDIT CARD INFORMATION

Mastercard ☐   Visa ☐   AmEx ☐   Discover ☐   Other ☐

Acct No: _____   Website: _____

Online Username: _____   Password: _____

Notes: _____

Mastercard ☐   Visa ☐   AmEx ☐   Discover ☐   Other ☐

Acct No: _____   Website: _____

Online Username: _____   Password: _____

Notes:

_____

Mastercard ☐   Visa ☐   AmEx ☐   Discover ☐   Other ☐

Acct No: _____   Website: _____

Online Username: _____   Password: _____

Notes: _____

Mastercard ☐   Visa ☐   AmEx ☐   Discover ☐   Other ☐

Acct No: _____   Website: _____

Online Username: _____   Password: _____

Notes: _____

Mastercard ☐   Visa ☐   AmEx ☐   Discover ☐   Other ☐

Acct No: _____   Website: _____

Online Username: _____   Password: _____

Notes: _____

Mastercard ☐   Visa ☐   AmEx ☐   Discover ☐   Other ☐

Acct No: _____   Website: _____

Online Username: _____   Password: _____

Notes: _____

Mastercard ☐   Visa ☐   AmEx ☐   Discover ☐   Other ☐

Acct No: _____   Website: _____

Online Username: _____   Password: _____

Notes: _____

Mastercard ☐   Visa ☐   AmEx ☐   Discover ☐   Other ☐

Acct No: _____   Website: _____

Online Username: _____   Password: _____

Notes: _____

Store Credit Card: _____

Acct No: _____

Online Username: _____ Password: _____

Notes: _____

Store Credit Card: _____

Acct No: _____

Online Username: _____ Password: _____

Notes: _____

Store Credit Card: _____

Acct No: _____

Online Username: _____ Password: _____

Notes: _____

Store Credit Card: _____

Acct No: _____

Online Username: _____ Password: _____

Notes: _____

Store Credit Card: _____

Acct No: _____

Online Username: _____ Password: _____

Notes: _____

Store Credit Card: _____

Acct No: _____

Online Username: _____   Password: _____

Notes: _____

Store Credit Card: _____

Acct No: _____

Online Username: _____   Password: _____

Notes: _____

INVESTMENTS: STOCKS, BONDS, MORE

Description: _____

Account No: _____

Contact: _____

Notes: _____

Description: _____

Account No: _____

Contact: _____

Notes: _____

Description: _____

Account No: _____

Contact: _____

Notes: _____

Description: _____

Account No: _____

Contact: _____

Notes: _____

Description: _____

Account No: _____

Contact: _____

Notes: _____

Description: _____

Account No: _____

Contact: _____

Notes: _____

Description: _____

Account No: _____

Contact: _____

Notes: _____

Description: _____

Account No: _____

Contact: _____

Notes: _____

Additional Notes on Investments: _____

_____

_____

_____

_____

_____

_____

_____

_____

_____

_____

_____

OTHER ACCOUNTS: REWARDS, FREQUENT FLYERS, ETC.

Name of Account:_____

Information: _____

Name of Account:_____

Information:_____

Name of Account:_____

Information:_____

TAX RECORDS

Federal and State Records are Located:_____

Online Tax Acct: _____

Username: _____   Password: _____

Notes:_____

SAFE DEPOSIT BOX

Bank and Location:_____

Number: _____

Key Location: _____

Contents: _____

Notes: _____

_____

_____

WHAT I OWE

Mortgage:_____

Lender Name and Contact Info: _____

Account No: _____

Location of Papers:_____

Property Tax Info: _____

Home Loan:_____

Lender Name and Contact Info: _____

Account No: _____

Location of Papers:_____

Car Loan:_____

Lender Name and Contact Info: _____

Account No: _____

Location of Papers:_____

Student Loan:_____

Lender Name and Contact Info: _____

Account No: _____

Location of Papers:_____

Medical Bills:_____

Contact Info: _____

Account No: _____

Location of Papers:_____

Medical Bills:_____

Contact Info: _____

Account No: _____

Location of Papers:_____

Credit Card Bills:_____

Contact Info: _____

Account No: _____

Location of Papers:_____

Credit Card Bills:_____

Contact Info: _____

Account No: _____

Location of Papers:_____

Personal Loans:_____

Contact Info: _____

Account No: _____

Location of Papers:_____

Judgments:_____

Contact Info: _____

Account No: _____

Location of Papers:_____

Possessions:_____

Contact Info: _____

Account No: _____

Location of Papers:_____

Other:_____

Contact Info: _____

Account No: _____

Location of Papers:_____

Notes: _____

_____

_____

_____

_____

_____

_____

_____

_____

_____

_____

_____

_____

_____

_____

WHAT IS OWE TO ME

Personal Loans:_____

Contact Info: _____

Details: _____

Location of Papers:_____

Judgments:_____

Contact Info: _____

Details: _____

Location of Papers:_____

Possessions:_____

Contact Info: _____

Details: _____

Location of Papers: _____

Other: _____

Contact Info: _____

Details: _____

Location of Papers: _____

Chapter 11

Retirement Plans and Pensions

This Chapter describes my retirement plans and pension benefits. Notify the managing company or organization of my Zombification or Death. Then evaluate each plan for amounts due to my estate or survivors.   Consult a Professional if necessary for help.

Employer Retirement and Pension Plans

Company Contact Information	Description, Status of Plan, and Beneficiary	Account Number and Online Access	Location of Statements

Additional Notes

Individual Retirement Accounts and Plans

Financial Institution Contact Information	Description, Status of Plan, and Beneficiary	Account Number and Online Access	Location of Statements

Additional Notes

Chapter 12

Government Benefits

In this Chapter, you will find information about any federal or state government benefits that I either currently collect or expect in the future. These include any benefits for my family members and survivors.

Social Security Benefits

I have outlined my Social Security benefits below. Upon my incapacity or death, notify the Social Security Administration at 800-772-1213 or contact your local SSA office. You can locate the local office by calling the SSA number or checking the government listings in the phone book.

Review the status of my benefits and ask the SSA representative whether additional benefits are available to me or to my family. A one-time death benefit is normally available for qualifying survivors. Information, publications, and forms are available at the Social Security Administration website, www.ssa.gov.

Program Name	Account Name and SSN	Account Access, Status, and Payment	Location of Documents
Retirement			
Disability			
Supplemental Security Income (SSI)			
Family			

Survivor			

Other Government Benefits

Following is a list of any other government benefits that I currently receive or expect in the future. For each program, notify the program administrator of my Zombification or Death, review the status of my benefits, and discuss whether additional benefits are available to my family or to me.

Program Name and Contact Information	Program Description	Account Name and Identification	Account Access, Status, and Payment	Location of Documents

Chapter 13

Business Information

Yup I'm dead and you'll need to know about my Employer and Business. Find info here.

Employer:_____

Position, Dates and Info:_____

_____

_____

Other Employers, Positions, Info:_____

_____

_____

_____

My Business Name:_____

Type of Business: _____

Location: _____

Contact Info: _____

Landlord:_____

Keys are Located: _____

Lease is Located:_____

Partners:_____

Corporate Docs Location: _____

Percentage of Ownership:_____

Disposition of Business (Continue/Transfer/Sell/Liquidate):_____

_____

Employees: _____

_____

Contact Info: _____

Contact Info: _____

Contact Info: _____

Accountant: _____

Contact Information: _____

_____

Attorney: _____

Contact Information: _____

_____

Insurance: _____

Contact Information: _____

_____

Bank: _____

Contact Information: _____

_____

Business Financial Records Location: _____

_____

Business Credit Card Information: _____

_____

Information on key customers, income from royalties, licenses, etc. _____

_____

_____

_____

Utilities and other Expenses: _____

_____

_____

_____

Assets with Details/Location of Documents, etc:_____

_____

_____

_____

Liabilities with Details/Location of Documents, etc:_____

_____

_____

_____

Business Website Information: _____

_____

_____

Business Social Media Sites

Name: _____

Username:_____ Password: _____

Name: _____

Username:_____ Password: _____

Name: _____

Username:_____ Password: _____

Other Notes and Instructions about the Business: _____

_____

_____

_____

_____

_____

_____

_____

_____

_____

_____

_____

_____

_____

_____

Chapter 14
Memberships and Organizations

In this Chapter you will find a list of clubs, groups and organizations to which I belong. You may need this information to notify others that I'm Dead, to complete my obituary, or cancel memberships.

Organization Name:_____

Contact Info: _____

Position Held: _____

Member #/Username:_____ Password: _____

Additional Notes: _____

_____

_____

Organization Name:_____

Contact Info: _____

Position Held: _____

Member #/Username:_____ Password: _____

Additional Notes: _____

_____

_____

Organization Name:_____

Contact Info: _____

Position Held: _____

Member #/Username:_____ Password: _____

Additional Notes: _____

_____

_____

Organization Name:_____

Contact Info: _____

Position Held: _____

Member #/Username:_____ Password: _____

Additional Notes: _____

_____

_____

Organization Name:_____

Contact Info: _____

Position Held: _____

Member #/Username:_____ Password: _____

Additional Notes: _____

_____

_____

Organization Name:_____

Contact Info: _____

Position Held: _____

Member #/Username:_____ Password: _____

Additional Notes: _____

_____

Organization Name:_____

Contact Info: _____

Position Held: _____

Member #/Username:_____ Password: _____

Additional Notes: _____

_____

_____

Organization Name:_____

Contact Info: _____

Position Held: _____

Member #/Username:_____ Password: _____

Additional Notes: _____

_____

_____

Organization Name:_____

Contact Info: _____

Position Held: _____

Chapter 15
Beneficiaries

What Beneficiaries Can Expect

LIFE INSURANCE POLICIES

Type of Policy:_____

Account No: _____

Contact Information: _____

Amount: _____

Beneficiary: _____

Location of Papers/Policy: _____

Notes: _____

_____

Type of Policy:_____

Account No: _____

Contact Information: _____

Amount: _____

Beneficiary: _____

Location of Papers/Policy: _____

Notes: _____

_____

Type of Policy:_____

Account No: _____

Contact Information: _____

Amount: _____

Beneficiary: _____

Location of Papers/Policy: _____

Notes: _____

_____

Type of Policy:_____

Account No: _____

Contact Information: _____

Amount: _____

Beneficiary: _____

Location of Papers/Policy: _____

Notes: _____

_____

Type of Policy:_____

Account No: _____

Contact Information: _____

Amount: _____

Beneficiary: _____

Location of Papers/Policy: _____

Notes: _____

EMPLOYER BENEFITS

Name:_____

Account No: _____

Contact Information: _____

Location of Papers/Policy: _____

Notes: _____

_____

SOCIAL SECURITY

Name:_____

Account No: _____

Contact Information: _____

Location of Papers/Policy: _____

Notes: _____

_____

RETIREMENT

Retirement Account: _____

Name:_____

Account No: _____

Contact Information: _____

Location of Papers/Policy: _____

Notes: _____

Retirement Account: _____

Name: _____

Account No: _____

Contact Information: _____

Location of Papers/Policy: _____

Notes: _____

_____

Retirement Account: _____

Name: _____

Account No: _____

Contact Information: _____

Location of Papers/Policy: _____

Notes: _____

_____

Retirement Account: _____

Name: _____

Account No: _____

Contact Information: _____

Location of Papers/Policy: _____

Notes: _____

_____

Additional Notes: _____

VETERAN'S BENEFITS

Veteran's Affairs Regional Office: _____

_____

Account No: _____

Contact Information: _____

Location of Papers/Policy: _____

Notes: _____

_____

_____

Other Notes: _____

_____

_____

_____

_____

_____

_____

_____

_____

_____

_____

Chapter 16
Personal Property

My Diggs, Rides and Belongings

REAL ESTATE

Residence:_____

Address: _____

_____

Co-Owner(s):_____

Location of Legal Docs: _____

_____

Location of Keys: _____

Location of Furnishing/Appliance Warranties, etc: _____

_____

Home Security Comp Contact Info: _____

_____

Notes: _____

_____

_____

If Renting Property, Location of Lease:_____

Lease Expires: _____

Location of Keys: _____

Property Manager Contact Info: _____

_____

Notes: _____

_____

_____

#2 - Second Home, Condo, Land, etc: (specify):_____

Address: _____

_____

Co-Owner(s):_____

_____

Location of Legal Documents: _____

Location of Keys: _____

Location of Furnishing/Appliance Warranties, etc: _____

Notes: _____

_____

_____

#3 - Second Home, Condo, Land, etc: (specify):_____

Address: _____

_____

Co-Owner(s):_____

_____

Location of Legal Documents: _____

Location of Keys: _____

Location of Furnishing/Appliance Warranties, etc: _____

Notes: _____

_____

_____

#4 - Second Home, Condo, Land, etc: (specify):_____

Address: _____

_____

Co-Owner(s):_____

_____

Location of Legal Documents: _____

Location of Keys: _____

Location of Furnishing/Appliance Warranties, etc: _____

Notes: _____

_____

_____

#5 - Second Home, Condo, Land, etc: (specify):_____

Address: _____

_____

Co-Owner(s):_____

_____

Location of Legal Documents: _____

Location of Keys: _____

Location of Furnishing/Appliance Warranties, etc: _____

Notes: _____

_____

Commercial Property:_____

Address: _____

_____

Co-Owner(s):_____

_____

Location of Legal Documents: _____

Location of Keys: _____

Location of Furnishing/Appliance Warranties, etc: _____

Notes: _____

_____

_____

Commercial Property:_____

Address: _____

_____

Co-Owner(s):_____

_____

Location of Legal Documents: _____

Location of Keys: _____

Location of Furnishing/Appliance Warranties, etc: _____

Notes: _____

_____

VEHICLES: CARS, BOATS AND MORE

Vehicle:_____

Year/Make/Model/Color: _____

_____

VIN:_____

Location of Title: _____

Location of Lease/Loan Information: _____

Location of Keys: _____

Notes: _____

_____

Vehicle:_____

Year/Make/Model/Color: _____

_____

VIN:_____

Location of Title: _____

Location of Lease/Loan Information: _____

Location of Keys: _____

Notes: _____

_____

Vehicle:_____

Year/Make/Model/Color: _____

_____

VIN:_____

Location of Title: _____

Location of Lease/Loan Information: _____

Location of Keys: _____

Notes: _____

_____

Vehicle:_____

Year/Make/Model/Color: _____

_____

VIN:_____

Location of Title: _____

Location of Lease/Loan Information: _____

Location of Keys: _____

Notes: _____

_____

Vehicle:_____

Year/Make/Model/Color: _____

_____

VIN:_____

Location of Title: _____

Location of Lease/Loan Information: _____

Location of Keys: _____

Notes: _____

_____

HEIRLOOMS AND PERSONAL ITEMS

Item: _____

Location: _____

Notes and Instructions: _____

_____

Item: _____

Location: _____

Notes and Instructions: _____

_____

Item: _____

Location: _____

Notes and Instructions: _____

_____

Item: _____

Location: _____

Notes and Instructions: _____

Item:_____

Location: _____

Notes and Instructions: _____

_____

Item:_____

Location: _____

Notes and Instructions: _____

_____

Item:_____

Location: _____

Notes and Instructions: _____

_____

Item:_____

Location: _____

Notes and Instructions: _____

_____

Item:_____

Location: _____

Notes and Instructions: _____

_____

FIREARMS

Location: _____

Registration and Information: _____

_____

Permit Information: _____

_____

Notes: _____

_____

_____

_____

Location: _____

Registration and Information: _____

_____

Permit Information: _____

_____

Notes: _____

_____

_____

_____

STORAGE UNIT(S)

Location: _____

Storage Company: _____

_____

Contact Information: _____

_____

Unit Number(s): _____

Contents: _____

_____

_____

Location of Key(s): _____

_____

Notes: _____

_____

_____

_____

SAFE

Location: _____

Location of Keys: _____

Combination: _____

_____

HIDDEN VALUABLES

Yes_____   **No** _____

If yes, information on their location may be found in my safe or safe deposit box._____

_____

_____

Safe Deposit Boxes

Bank Name and Contact Information	People With Authorized Access	Box Number and Location of Keys	Description of Contents

Info about Safe Deposit Boxes:

If I am incapacitated. If I am incapacitated and you co-own a safe deposit box with me, your access rights are unaffected. If you do not already have access, however, you will need to meet special requirements before the financial institution will open a safe deposit box for you.

- If you are my agent for finances under a durable power of attorney, you will need to present the power of attorney document. If the document is a "springing" power of attorney, you will also need to present doctors' statements to verify that I am incapacitated.
- If you do not meet these requirements, you will need to obtain a court order to access a safe deposit box.

Now that I'm dead, you will need to meet these special requirements before the financial institution will open a safe deposit box for you.

- If you are a co-owner on the box, your access will continue unimpeded unless the box is temporarily sealed (see below).
- If you are my executor or successor trustee, you will need to present a certified copy of my death certificate and a copy of the will or trust that names you to the job. (There may be a few weeks' delay, if the box is temporarily sealed. Again, see below.)
- If you meet none of these requirements, you will need to obtain a court order to access the safe deposit box.

Note that in some states, safe deposit boxes are sealed for a few weeks following the death of the owner so the state taxing authority can review the contents. During this time, you will not be able to obtain access to the box without a court order.

Other Notes: _____

_____

_____

_____

_____

_____

_____

_____

_____

_____

_____

_____

_____

Chapter 17
Insurance

All About Insurance

Life Insurance: _____

Agent Name: _____

Contact Info: _____

_____

Location of Policy: _____

Homeowner's Insurance: _____

Agent Name: _____

Contact Info: _____

_____

Location of Policy: _____

Rental Insurance: _____

Agent Name: _____

Contact Info: _____

_____

Location of Policy: _____

Health Insurance: _____

Insurer Name: _____

Contact Info: _____

_____

Health Savings Account (HAS) Information: _____

_____

Medicare/Medicaid:_____

Account Number: _____

Contact Info: _____

_____

Dental Insurance:_____

Insurer Name: _____

Contact Info: _____

_____

Vision Insurance:_____

Insurer Name: _____

Contact Info: _____

_____

Motor Vehicle Insurance:_____

Insurer Name: _____

Contact Info: _____

_____

Location of Policy: _____

_____

Notes: _____

_____

_____

_____

_____

Other Insurance: _____

Insurer Name: _____

Contact Info: _____

_____

Location of Policy: _____

_____

Notes: _____

_____

_____

Chapter 18

What to Pay, Close, Cancel

In this section, you'll find information about what accounts can be paid, closed or canceled.

CREDIT CARDS
(See Chapter 10)

UTILITIES

Gas/Propane/Oil Provider:_____

Contact Information: _____

Electric Provider: _____

Contact Information: _____

Water Provider: _____

Contact Information: _____

Phone (landline) Number: _____

Phone (landline) Provider: _____

Contact Information: _____

Cell Phone Number: _____

Cell Phone Provider:_____

Contact Information: _____

Cable TV Provider: _____

Account Number: _____

Contact Information: _____

ONLINE RETAIL ACCOUNTS

Account Name: _____

Username: _____ Password: _____

Notes: _____

_____

Account Name: _____

Username: _____ Password: _____

Notes: _____

_____

Account Name: _____

Username: _____ Password: _____

Notes: _____

_____

Account Name: _____

Username: _____ Password: _____

Notes: _____

_____

OTHER ONLINE ACCOUNTS

Account Name: _____

Username: _____   Password: _____

Notes: _____

_____

Account Name: _____

Username: _____   Password: _____

Notes: _____

_____

Account Name: _____

Username: _____   Password: _____

Notes: _____

_____

Account Name: _____

Username: _____   Password: _____

Notes: _____

_____

Account Name: _____

Username: _____   Password: _____

Notes: _____

_____

AUTOPAY ACCOUNTS

Account Name: _____

Username: _____   Password: _____

Notes: _____

_____

Account Name: _____

Username: _____   Password: _____

Notes: _____

_____

Account Name: _____

Username: _____   Password: _____

Notes: _____

_____

Account Name: _____

Username: _____   Password: _____

Notes: _____

_____

Account Name: _____

Username: _____ Password: _____

Notes: _____

_____

CHARITIES

Charity Name: _____

Contact Information: _____

_____

Charity Name: _____

Contact Information: _____

_____

Charity Name: _____

Contact Information: _____

_____

Charity Name: _____

Contact Information: _____

_____

Charity Name: _____

Contact Information: _____

Notes: _____

_____

_____

_____

SUBSCRIPTIONS: PRINT PUBLICATIONS, EMAIL NEWSLETTERS, ETC.

Publication Name: _____

Contact Information: _____

_____

Publication Name: _____

Contact Information: _____

_____

Publication Name: _____

Contact Information: _____

_____

Publication Name: _____

Contact Information: _____

_____

Publication Name: _____

Contact Information: _____

Notes: _____

_____

_____

_____

MEMBERSHIPS

Organization Name: _____

Contact Information: _____

_____

Organization Name: _____

Contact Information: _____

_____

Organization Name: _____

Contact Information: _____

_____

Organization Name: _____

Contact Information: _____

_____

Organization Name: _____

Contact Information: _____

_____

Notes: _____

_____

_____

_____

OTHERS TO PAY, CLOSE, CANCEL

_____

_____

_____

_____

_____

_____

_____

_____

_____

_____

_____

Chapter 19

EMAIL AND SOCIAL MEDIA

Consider saving important emails, favorite photos, etc.

EMAIL

Email Account: _____

Username: _____

Password: _____

Notes: _____

_____

Email Account: _____

Username:_____

Password: _____

Notes: _____

_____

Email Account: _____

Username: _____

Password: _____

Notes:_____

SOCIAL MEDIA

Facebook: _____

Username: _____

Password: _____

Notes: _____

_____

LinkedIn: _____

Username: _____

Password: _____

Notes: _____

_____

Twitter: _____

Username: _____

Password: _____

Notes: _____

_____

Instagram: _____

Username: _____

Password: _____

Notes: _____

Other: _____

Username: _____

Password: _____

Notes: _____

_____

Other: _____

Username: _____

Password: _____

Notes: _____

_____

Other: _____

Username: _____

Password: _____

Notes: _____

_____

Other:_____

Username: _____

Password: _____

Notes: _____

_____

My Website or Blog: _____

Username:_____   Password: _____

Webmasters: _____

Contact Info: _____

Domain Hosting Info: _____

Notes: _____

_____

_____

Chapter 20

Secure Places and Passwords

This section provides the information you will need to access property that I manage or store in secured places—including online accounts with passwords, physical items secured with combination locks, access codes, or keys, safe deposit boxes, and secret locations.

Products, Services, and Passwords

Product or Service	Account Name, User Name, or Account Number	Password, Combination, or PIN	Location of Key

Common Passwords

Here are some of my common passwords:			

Additional Notes

Chapter 21
Organ or Body Donation

Now that I'm dead, If I have chosen to donate my body, organs, or tissues, I have indicated so here. Please review this section along with Chapters 22-25 prior to making my final arrangements.

After my death, I want to donate my body, organs, or tissues:　　[ ]　Yes　　[ ]　No

If "No," skip the rest of this section and turn to the next section.

Wishes for Donation

I would like to donate:	[ ]　My body
	[ ]　Any needed organs or tissues
	[ ]　Only the following organs or tissues:

Arrangements for Donation

Receiving Organization's Name and Contact Info	
Location of Documents	
Additional Notes	

Chapter 22

Burial or Cremation

In this section, I have outlined my wishes and any arrangements I have made for my burial or cremation.

I have selected either _____ Burial or _____ Cremation and have provided details about my wishes.

Insurance Policy for Funeral/Burial expenses: _____

_____

Contact Information: _____

_____

Funeral Home: _____

_____

Contact Information: _____

_____

Disposal of Remains:

I have _____ or have not _____ made arrangements with this organization.

Burial Organization: _____ _____

Contact Information: _____

_____

Burial Location and Contact Information:_____

_____

Location of Documents:_____

Cemetery:_____

Head Stone:_____

_____

_____

Contact Info for Cemetery:_____

Plot #: _____

Additional Notes: _____

_____

_____

I have _____ or have not _____ made arrangements with this organization.

Cremation: _____

Ashes to be Scattered/In-ground/ To Individual: _____

_____

_____

Cremation Organization Contact Info: _____

_____

Location of Documents:_____

Additional Notes: _____

Casket or Urn:

I have _____ or have not _____ made arrangements with the following organization:

_____

_____

I would like a Casket/Urn or Other Container to hold my remains: _____

_____

_____

Material (Wood/Metal/Other):_____ _____

_____

Cost Range (Economical/Moderate/Luxury):_____

_____

Additional Notes/Details: _____

_____

Headstone, Monument or Burial Marker:

I have _____ or have not _____ made arrangements with the following organization:

_____

_____

I would like a Headstone/Monument/Marker: _____

_____

Material:_____

_____

Design: _____

_____

Inscription: _____

_____

_____

Finish: _____

Cost Range (Economical/Moderate/Luxury):_____

_____

Additional Notes/Details: _____

_____

Burial or Cremation Apparel:

I wish to specify burial or cremation apparel and accessories _____ YES _____ NO

Clothing, Accessory, or Other Item	Location	Remove Before Interment or Cremation	
		[ ] Yes	[ ] No
		[ ] Yes	[ ] No
		[ ] Yes	[ ] No

		[ ] Yes	[ ] No
		[ ] Yes	[ ] No
		[ ] Yes	[ ] No

Additional Notes on Clothing, Accessories, Appearance (makeup/hair):

_____

_____

_____

_____

_____

_____

_____

_____

_____

_____

_____

_____

_____

_____

_____

Chapter 23

Funeral and Memorial Services

In this section, I have outlined my wishes and any arrangements I have made for services or ceremonies after my death. Please review this section along with Chapters 21, 22, 24, 25 prior to making my final arrangements.

Viewing, Visitation, or Wake

I would like a viewing, visitation, or wake: [   ] Yes   [   ] No

Type of Service	
Location and Contact Information	
Existing Arrangements and Location of Documents	

Body Present [ ] Yes [ ] No	**Casket** [ ] Yes [ ] No	**Casket** [ ] Open [ ] Closed

Invitees [ ] Public [ ] Private	**Timing and Days/Hours**
Special Requests	

Additional Notes	

Funeral or Memorial Service

I would like a funeral or memorial: [   ] Yes   [   ] No

Location and Contact Information	
Existing Arrangements and Location of Documents	

Body and Casket Present	**Casket**	**Other Items**
[ ] Yes [ ] No	[ ] Open [ ] Closed	[ ] Photo—Location: [ ] Other: _____
Flowers	**Invitees**	**Timing and Days/Hours**
	[ ] Public [ ] Private	

Type of Service	Service Contact	Facilitator
[ ] Religious [ ] Military [ ] Other	Name Contact Information	Name Contact Information

Notes:

Eulogy

Name	Name	Name
Contact Information	Contact Information	Contact Information

Music Selections and Musicians

Readings

Pallbearers

Name #1	Name #2	Name #3
Contact Information	Contact Information	Contact Information
Name #4	Name #5	Name #6
Contact Information	Contact Information	Contact Information
Name #7	Name #8	Name-Alternate
Contact Information	Contact Information	Contact Information
Name-Alternate	Name-Alternate	Name-Alternate
Contact Information	Contact Information	Contact Information

Graveside Ceremony	Transportation to Service
[ ] Graveside only [ ] Following funeral [ ] None	

Additional Notes	

Reception or Celebration of Life

I would like a reception or celebration of life: [ ] Yes   [ ] No

Location and Contact Information	

Existing Arrangements and Location of Documents	

Invitees [ ] Public [ ] Private	**Food and Drink**	

Additional Notes	

Chapter 24
Obituary

You will find details regarding my Obituary in this Chapter

Please publish my obituary.   [   ] Yes   [   ] No

I have already drafted an obituary: [   ] Yes   (Location: _____

_____)   [   ] No I have not drafted an Obituary.

If I have not drafted an obituary, please prepare one using the information and instructions below.

Obituary Overview

Obituary Length	[ ] Brief [ ] Moderate [ ] Article Length
Photographs	[ ] Yes (Location: _____) [ ] No
Publications	

Obituary Details

Date and Place of Birth	
Military Service	
Spouse, Children, Grandchildren, Parents, Siblings	
Employment and Business Interests	

Memberships and Communities	
Education	
Awards and Achievements	
Interests and Hobbies	
Values	
Public or Private	See Funeral and Memorial Services - Chapter 23; (2) funeral or memorial service; and (3) reception or celebration of life.
Flowers	[ ] Yes. Send to:
	[ ] No. "No flowers, please."
	[ ] No. "In lieu of flowers, please send donations to [the organizations listed below]."
Donations or Remembrances (Organization and Contact Information)	
Other	

Chapter 25

Will and Trust

In this section, you will find important information about my will. If I have made other estate planning documents, such as a living trust, other trusts, or a marital property agreement, you will find those listed here as well.

If an attorney or other professional (such as a tax expert) helped me prepare a document listed here, I have included contact information for him or her. You can consult the listed professional if you have questions about the document or need help carrying out its terms.

Document Title	
Date Prepared	
Professional Help	An attorney or other professional helped me prepare this document: [ ] Yes [ ] No
Professional's Name, Title, and Contact Information	
Location of Original Document	
Locations of Copies of This Document	
Executor or Successor Trustee	
Alternate 1	
Alternate 2	

Additional Notes	
Document Title	
Date Prepared	
Professional Help	An attorney or other professional helped me prepare this document: [ ] Yes [ ] No
Professional's Name, Title, and Contact Information	
Location of Original Document	
Locations of Copies of This Document	
Executor or Successor Trustee	
Alternate 1	
Alternate 2	
Additional Notes	

Document Title	
Date Prepared	
Professional Help	An attorney or other professional helped me prepare this document: [ ] Yes [ ] No
Professional's Name, Title, and Contact Information	
Location of Original Document	
Locations of Copies of This Document	
Executor or Successor Trustee	
Alternate 1	
Alternate 2	
Additional Notes	

Document Title	
Date Prepared	
Professional Help	An attorney or other professional helped me prepare this document: [ ] Yes [ ] No

Professional's Name, Title, and Contact Information	
Location of Original Document	
Locations of Copies of This Document	
Executor or Successor Trustee	
Alternate 1	

Chapter 26

MISCELLANEOUS INFORMATION

If I am Zombified and unable to communicate, this is what I would like my caregivers to know:

_____

_____

_____

_____

_____

_____

_____

_____

_____

_____

_____

_____

_____

The people listed below have been told about this book:

Name:_____

Contact Information: _____

_____

_____

Name:_____

Contact Information: _____

_____

_____

Name:_____

Contact Information: _____

_____

_____

Name:_____

Contact Information: _____

_____

_____

Name:_____

Contact Information: _____

_____

OTHER NOTES:

_____

_____

_____

_____

_____

_____

_____

_____

_____

_____

_____

_____

_____

_____

_____

_____

_____

Chapter 27

MISCELLANEOUS CONTACTS

_____

_____

_____

_____

_____

_____

_____

_____

_____

_____

_____

_____

_____

_____

_____

Chapter 28

SERVICE PROVIDERS

My current service providers are listed below. This information may help you manage bills and expenses or provide ongoing care for me, my home, or my other property. Over time, you should cancel or modify these service arrangements, as necessary.

Name and Contact Information	Type of Care and Details

Chapter 29

MY PERSONAL WISHES

_____

_____

_____

_____

_____

_____

_____

_____

_____

_____

_____

_____

_____

Chapter 30

LAST WORDS

_____

_____

_____

_____

_____

_____

_____

_____

_____

_____

_____

_____

Signed,

_____

Name and Date